Jock the pocket

J

This fuzzbuzz is called Jock the pocket.

He has a red bonnet with a blue pom-pom.

He is called Jock the pocket because of his big brown pocket.

His pocket has a red ribbon and a big red zip.

The big fuzzbuzzes from the clan are very happy to see Jock.

They love to see him coming because his pocket is full of letters.

The fuzzbuzzes of the clan Macfuzz love to write letters.

They hand these letters to Jock.

He goes to all the crofts with them.

Macfuzz
the buzz
Macfuzz the buzz
The glen Macfuzz
Scotland

Jock has a letter for the chief of the clan.

The chief is called Macfuzz the buzz.

Jock drops the letter into his letter box.

This is the letter.

Can you read it?

> The glen Macfuzz
> Scotland
>
> Can Macfuzz the buzz and the clan come to have dinner with Hilda?
> There is some haggis for you all.
>
> love from
> Hilda Ⓗ

The glen
The gle

Macfuzz the buzz picks up his letter.

He is going to read it.

He is very happy because all fuzzbuzzes love to go out for dinner.

He is going to write back to Hilda so first of all he gets out some black ink.

This is the letter Macfuzz writes.

Can you read all the words?

> The glen Macfuzz
> Scotland
>
> The chief of the clan and all his fuzzbuzzes can come to have dinner with you.
>
> Macfuzz the buzz Ⓜ

Macfuzz gives this letter to Jock.

Jock puts it into his pocket.

Now he can go back to Hilda.

Where are all the little fuzzbuzzes?
The sun is out so all the little fuzzbuzzes have come out to play.
Can you see them?
They are under the trees next to the river Mac.
But they are not happy.
They are fed up.
They are so fed up that they are going off to hunt for Jock.
It is fun to play with Jock.
They love it.

Draw some little fuzzbuzzes under a tree.

Write

The little fuzzbuzzes are fed up.

J

The little fuzzbuzzes love to see Jock because of his big brown pocket.

This pocket is astonishing.

It has a red ribbon and a red zip.

But they are not astonishing.

His pocket is astonishing because it is full of astonishing things.

It is full of all the things that the little fuzzbuzzes love.

Jock just puts his hand into his pocket and pulls things out.

This is not a trick.

It is just astonishing.

Draw and colour this pocket.

Write

This pocket is astonishing.

It is full of good things.

glen Macfuzz
J

The little fuzzbuzzes go as fast as they can to see Jock.

They get there at last.

Jock has just come down from the hills.

He is ready for them.

He is not mad at them.

He is not upset and he is not grumpy.

He is happy to see them all.

He puts his hand into his pocket and out comes a big stick of rock.

Can you read the words in it?

Draw the rock and colour it in.

Write the words in it.

Write

Jock gives them this stick of rock.

Jock puts his hand back into his pocket.

Now he pulls out a tin and a pin.

Next, he pulls out a fan and a van.

He drops these things onto the grass.

Draw and colour these things.

Write

Jock gives them a pin and a tin, a fan and a van.

Next, he pulls out some more things.
A cup and a mop and a blue and red top.

A net and a jet come out next.

Draw and colour these things.

Write

Now they get a cup, a mop, a net, a jet and a top.

Jock pulls still more things from
his astonishing pocket.

He pulls out a frog on a log.

Can you see it?

Can you see two boots and an
umbrella?

Can you see a vest, a kilt and a cap?

Can you see a gun?

They are all on the green grass.

In the end Jock gives them all
an apple and an orange.

Draw a frog on a log.

**Draw some more of the things
that Jock pulls out.**

Now the little fuzzbuzzes are not fed up.

They are very happy.

They are so happy that they write out some words for Jock.

They are going to sing them to him.

Can you read the words that they are going to sing for him?

The things we love,
The things we love,
Jock the pocket has them.
A fan and a van,
A frog on a log,
Jock the pocket has them.
A cup and a mop,
A blue and red top,
Jock the pocket has them.

W
T
A

Windbag comes out now.
He has his bagpipes with him.
He is going to play them.
The little fuzzbuzzes get into a ring.
Now they can sing for Jock.
Don the bonnet, Big Ben, Black Angus, and Tosh come across to see the fun.

Write

Now the little fuzzbuzzes sing for Jock.

J

Jock is very very happy.
He pulls out some more things from his astonishing pocket.
He pulls out a duck first.
Next he pulls out a ring.
Now a little well comes out.

Draw these things.

Write

Jock gives them a duck, a ring and a well.

Now more things come out.

Down they all come.

Now more and more and more
things come out.

Jock just cannot stop.

They still come down.

Jock just goes on and on and on.

In the end, Jock has to stop.
He cannot go on.
He goes into his yellow and brown croft.
He is going to have a sleep.
Can you see all the things on the grass?
They have all come from his astonishing pocket.
The little fuzzbuzzes are very happy.
Now they are not fed up.
There is something for them all.
A little fuzzbuzz creeps under all the things.
Can you see a fuzzbuzz on top of the things?
They are all very very happy.

Write this out and write in the missing words.

Hilda writes a letter to ______ .

They can have ______ for dinner.

The little fuzzbuzzes are ______ up.

Jock has an astonishing ______ .

Jock gives them a stick of ______ .

He pulls out a red and blue ______ .